Shifting Borders: Eastern Europe's Turbulent Journey Through World War II

Copyright Page

TITLE: Shifting Borders: Eastern Europe's Turbulent Journey Through World War II

1ST Edition

Copyright @ 2023

ISBN: 9798223876243

Shifting Borders: Eastern Europe' Turbulent Journey Through World War II

By Roberto Miguel Rodriguez

Chapter 1: Under Several Flags: A Historical Account of Cities and Countries that Changed Hands Several Times During World War

- Introduction to the concept of shifting borders and its impact on Eastern Europe during World War II

- Overview of major cities and countries that experienced multiple occupations

- Importance of studying this aspect of history for a comprehensive understanding of the war

Chapter 2: Cities and countries in Eastern Europe that changed hands multiple times during World War II

- Detailed exploration of specific cities and regions that were heavily contested

- Analysis of the strategic importance of these areas and the reasons behind frequent changes in ownership

- Examination of the military strategies employed by different factions to gain control

Chapter 3: The impact of multiple occupations on major European cities during World War II

- Study of the cultural and social impact on local populations

- Exploration of the challenges faced by civilians living in areas that were frequently occupied

- Analysis of the role of resistance movements and their contribution to the war effort

Chapter 4: The economic consequences of frequent changes in ownership during World War II

- Examination of the economic disruptions caused by shifting borders

- Analysis of the long-term effects on trade, industry, and infrastructure

- Case studies of specific cities and regions to illustrate the economic consequences

Chapter 5: The long-term effects of multiple occupations on the political landscape of cities and countries in the post-war era

- Exploration of how shifting borders shaped the political landscape of Eastern Europe after the war

- Analysis of the challenges faced in rebuilding and establishing stable governments

- Examination of the lingering tensions and conflicts resulting from the multiple occupations

Conclusion: The lasting legacy of shifting borders in Eastern Europe during World War II

- Summary of the key findings and insights from the book

- Reflection on the enduring impact of multiple occupations on the region

- Consideration of the lessons learned and their relevance to contemporary conflicts

By expanding upon these chapters and sub-chapters with more detailed information and analysis, "Shifting Borders: Eastern Europe's Turbulent Journey through World War II" aims to provide a comprehensive understanding of the impact of multiple occupations on cities and countries in Eastern Europe during the war. This book is intended for historians, educators, students, and the general public interested in gaining a deeper insight into this pivotal period in history.

Chapter 1: UNDER SEVERAL FLAGS: A HISTORICAL ACCOUNT OF CITIES AND COUNTRIES THAT CHANGED HANDS SEVERAL TIMES DURING WORLD WAR II

Cities and countries in Eastern Europe that changed hands multiple times during World War II

Cities and countries in Eastern Europe were at the epicenter of the cataclysmic events that unfolded during World War II. These regions became a hotbed of conflict, as different factions vied for control and power. In "Shifting Borders: Eastern Europe's Turbulent Journey through World War II," we delve into the profound impact of multiple occupations on major cities and countries, shedding light on lesser-known regions that were heavily contested during this tumultuous period.

Throughout the war, cities such as Warsaw, Prague, and Budapest changed hands multiple times, witnessing the ebb and flow of power. The strategic importance of key ports and harbors, like Danzig and Odessa, made them prime targets, resulting in frequent capture and recapture. These cities and regions became battlefields as opposing forces employed various military strategies to gain control.

One aspect we explore in detail is the role of resistance movements in cities and countries that experienced frequent occupation. These courageous individuals fought against the occupiers, often at great personal risk, striving to reclaim their freedom and protect their cultural heritage.

The impact of recurring occupations on local populations cannot be overstated. Civilians faced immense challenges, enduring hardships, displacement, and loss of life. The cultural and social fabric of these communities was deeply affected, as the occupying forces imposed their ideologies and customs on the local populace.

Moreover, the economic consequences of these frequent changes in ownership were severe. Infrastructure was often destroyed, resources were depleted, and trade was disrupted, leaving the cities and countries in a state of economic turmoil.

As the war drew to a close, the long-term effects of multiple occupations on the political landscape became apparent. The post-war era saw a reshaping of borders, the emergence of new nations, and the establishment of political systems influenced by the experiences endured during the war.

"Shifting Borders" offers a comprehensive exploration of these topics, providing a historical account that will captivate historians, educators, students, and the public alike. By delving into the challenges faced by civilians, the military strategies employed, and the enduring legacy of these occupations, this subchapter sheds light on a lesser-known aspect of World War II, enriching our understanding of this tumultuous period in Eastern Europe's history.

Poland: A Nation in Turmoil

During World War II, Poland found itself thrust into the heart of the conflict, becoming a nation in turmoil as it experienced multiple occupations and changing borders. This subchapter delves into the profound impact of these events on the country, addressing the historical, social, economic, and political consequences that shaped Poland's trajectory.

One cannot discuss Poland's turbulent journey without acknowledging the strategic importance it held for both the Axis and Allied powers. Its geographic location made it a coveted prize, resulting in fierce battles and frequent changes in ownership. Major cities such as Warsaw, Krakow, and Gdansk became hotbeds of conflict, witnessing multiple occupations and enduring the devastating effects of war.

The subchapter also sheds light on the resilience of the Polish people, exploring their active role in resistance movements. Despite the constant threat of occupation, Poles formed underground networks, undertaking acts of sabotage and espionage to oppose their oppressors. The courage and determination of these resistance fighters played a crucial role in the struggle for liberation.

Moreover, the subchapter delves into the cultural, social, and economic impact of recurring occupations on the local population. Polish society experienced immense hardship, with infrastructure destroyed, resources depleted, and communities uprooted. The consequences of these frequent changes in ownership were far-reaching, leaving a lasting imprint on the fabric of Polish society.

The long-term effects of Poland's tumultuous journey are also explored, particularly in the post-war era. The subchapter examines how multiple occupations shaped the political landscape of the country, influencing its alliances, government structure, and foreign policies. Poland emerged from the war with a new identity, forever changed by the trials it endured.

This subchapter will be of great significance to historians, educators, students, and the wider public. It will also cater to specific niches such as those interested in the impact of multiple occupations on major European cities, lesser-known regions heavily contested during the war, and the challenges faced by civilians living in frequently occupied areas. Furthermore, it will provide insights into the military strategies employed, the economic consequences, and the cultural and social implications of these recurrent occupations.

By examining Poland's tumultuous journey during World War II, this subchapter aims to illuminate the complexities of war and its enduring effects on nations caught in its midst. It serves as a testament to the indomitable spirit of the Polish people and their resilience in the face of overwhelming adversity.

Ukraine: Battleground of Nations

During World War II, Ukraine emerged as a key battleground for various nations, experiencing frequent changes in ownership as different factions vied for control. This subchapter titled "Ukraine: Battleground of Nations" explores the impact of multiple occupations on major European cities, the challenges faced by civilians living in these areas, and the long-term effects on the political landscape of Ukraine in the post-war era.

Cities and regions in Eastern Europe, including Ukraine, were heavily contested during World War II. The strategic importance of key ports and harbors, such as Odessa and Sevastopol, made them prime targets for capture by different factions. These cities became a focal point for military strategies employed by various nations, resulting in intense battles and significant loss of life.

The recurring occupations had a profound cultural and social impact on the local populations. Civilians faced numerous challenges as their cities changed hands multiple times. They had to cope with the constant presence of occupying forces, endure economic hardships, and navigate the complex web of political allegiances. Resistance movements played a crucial role in these cities and regions, providing hope and support to those living under occupation.

The economic consequences of frequent changes in ownership were severe. Industries were disrupted, infrastructure was damaged, and resources were depleted. The constant upheaval hindered economic development and stability, leaving a lasting impact on the region's prosperity.

The long-term effects of multiple occupations on the political landscape of Ukraine were significant. The shifting borders and allegiances during the war laid the groundwork for the post-war era. The scars of occupation and the struggle for independence shaped the political discourse, leading to a complex and contested political landscape in the years that followed.

This subchapter aims to provide historians, educators, students, and the public with a comprehensive account of Ukraine's role as a battleground during World War II. By examining the impact on major cities, the challenges faced by civilians, and the long-term effects on politics and society, readers will gain a deeper understanding of the turbulent journey Eastern Europe experienced during this tumultuous period.

Belarus: Caught in the Crossfire

During World War II, the nation of Belarus found itself caught in the crossfire of warring factions, experiencing multiple occupations and changing hands several times. This subchapter explores the tumultuous journey of Belarus through this dark period in history, shedding light on the impact it had on the country and its people.

Belarus, strategically located in Eastern Europe, became a hotly contested region due to its key ports and harbors. Its significance as a transportation hub and vital link between major powers made it a prime target for both the Axis and Allied forces. As a result, cities and regions in Belarus such as Minsk, Brest, and Grodno became epicenters of intense fighting and frequent changes in ownership.

The repeated occupations had devastating consequences for the local population. Civilians living in these areas faced immense challenges, enduring the horrors of war, displacement, and the loss of loved ones. The cultural and social fabric of these communities was deeply impacted, as people had to navigate life under different rulers and adapt to varying ideologies.

Resistance movements played a crucial role in these cities and countries that changed hands multiple times. Partisans and underground networks fought fiercely against the occupiers, employing guerilla tactics and acts of sabotage to disrupt enemy operations. These acts of resistance not only provided hope for the local population but also contributed to the eventual liberation of Belarus.

The economic consequences of frequent changes in ownership were severe. Infrastructure was destroyed, industries were disrupted, and the agricultural sector suffered immensely. The constant upheaval hindered any chance of stability and hindered the country's ability to recover in the post-war era.

The impact of the multiple occupations extended beyond the war years. The political landscape of Belarus was forever altered, with new power structures emerging and old ones crumbling. The scars of occupation were etched deep into the collective memory of the Belarusian people, shaping their identity and influencing their political choices in the post-war era.

This subchapter delves into the lesser-known stories of Belarus, shining a light on the struggles faced by its people and the resilience they displayed in the face of adversity. It explores the military strategies employed by different factions, the challenges faced by civilians, and the long-term effects of the frequent changes in ownership. By understanding the experiences of Belarus during World War II, we gain a deeper insight into the broader impact of the war on Eastern Europe and the world at large.

Baltic States: A Constant Struggle

During World War II, the Baltic States - Estonia, Latvia, and Lithuania - faced a constant struggle as they found themselves caught in the crosshairs of various factions vying for control over Eastern Europe. This subchapter explores the turbulent journey of these nations, shedding light on the profound impact of multiple occupations on major European cities, the resilience of local populations, and the long-term consequences on the political landscape of the region.

The Baltic States, strategically positioned on the Eastern Front, became key targets for the Soviet Union, Germany, and later, the Allied forces. As a result, cities like Tallinn, Riga, and Vilnius changed hands multiple times, enduring devastating bombings, sieges, and occupation by different factions. These cities became battlegrounds, witnessing the horrors of war and the fierce struggles for dominance.

The recurring occupations had profound cultural, social, and economic consequences. Local populations faced constant upheaval, as their lives were disrupted by changing rulers, ideologies, and policies. Resistance movements emerged, bravely defying occupation forces and fighting for their nations' freedom. These movements played a crucial role in preserving national identity and inspiring hope amidst the chaos.

Furthermore, the frequent changes in ownership had severe economic implications. Infrastructure was destroyed, industries disrupted, and resources plundered. The Baltic States faced significant challenges in rebuilding their economies and recovering from the scars of war.

The military strategies employed by different factions to gain control of these cities and countries were diverse and complex. The Baltic States were not mere pawns in the larger chessboard of World War II; they were also strategic locations due to their key ports and harbors. The control of these ports was fiercely contested, as they provided crucial access to the Baltic Sea and the wider Eastern European region.

The long-term effects of these recurring occupations are still felt today. The political landscape of the Baltic States was fundamentally altered, with the Soviet Union ultimately establishing control over the region. The scars of occupation and the struggle for independence continue to shape these nations and their relationship with the rest of Europe.

In conclusion, the Baltic States faced a constant struggle during World War II, as they were repeatedly occupied by different factions. This subchapter delves into the impact of these occupations on major cities, the resilience of local populations, and the long-term consequences for the political landscape of the region. By understanding the challenges faced by these nations, we gain valuable insights into the complex history of Eastern Europe during this tumultuous period.

The impact of multiple occupations on major European cities during World War II

During World War II, major European cities became the battlegrounds for various factions, resulting in multiple occupations that had profound effects on the cities and their populations. This subchapter explores the consequences of these recurring occupations, including their cultural, social, economic, and political impacts.

Cities and countries in Eastern Europe were particularly affected, as they changed hands multiple times throughout the war. Lesser-known cities and regions that were heavily contested became the epicenters of conflict, with strategic importance placed on key ports and harbors that were repeatedly captured. These cities became crucial for supply routes and military operations, making them prime targets for both Axis and Allied forces.

The constant shifting of ownership had severe consequences for the local populations. Civilians living in these areas faced numerous challenges, including widespread destruction, displacement, and loss of life. Resistance movements played a crucial role in these cities and countries, as they fought against the occupiers and contributed to the eventual liberation.

The cultural and social impact of recurring occupations cannot be underestimated. Local populations experienced the imposition of different ideologies, languages, and customs, which often led to a clash of cultures. The long-term effects of these occupations can still be felt today, as they shaped the political landscape of these cities and countries in the post-war era.

Economically, frequent changes in ownership disrupted trade and commerce. Businesses were forced to adapt to constantly shifting regulations, and infrastructure suffered from the destruction caused by the occupying forces. The economic consequences of these occupations were far-reaching and continued to affect these cities and countries long after the war ended.

Military strategies employed by different factions to gain control of cities and countries were diverse and often brutal. The battles for these cities were fiercely fought, and the tactics used by both sides left lasting scars on the urban landscapes.

This subchapter aims to shed light on the often-overlooked aspects of World War II, focusing on the impact of multiple occupations on major European cities. By understanding the challenges faced by civilians, the strategies employed by military forces, and the long-term consequences of these occupations, historians, educators, students, and the public can gain a comprehensive understanding of the complexities of this turbulent period in history.

Warsaw: From Glory to Ruins

Warsaw, the capital of Poland, experienced a tragic transformation during World War II, going from a city of grandeur and prosperity to a city in ruins. This subchapter explores the journey of Warsaw, shedding light on the impact of multiple occupations and the resilience of its people.

As one of the cities that changed hands several times during the war, Warsaw became a strategic prize for both the Axis and Allied powers. Its strategic location in Eastern Europe made it a significant target, leading to intense battles and frequent shifts in control. The city's key ports and harbors played a crucial role in these power struggles, as they were repeatedly captured and recaptured.

The people of Warsaw endured unimaginable hardships throughout the war. They faced constant fear, as their city became a battleground for opposing forces. The local population experienced the cultural and social impact of recurring occupations, with their way of life constantly disrupted. The economic consequences were dire, as the frequent changes in ownership led to widespread destruction of infrastructure and resources.

However, amidst the chaos, Warsaw became a symbol of resistance. The city's brave inhabitants formed underground movements and fought back against the occupiers. The resistance movements played a significant role in the city's history, inspiring hope and preserving the spirit of freedom.

The challenges faced by civilians living in areas frequently occupied during the war were immense. They had to navigate through a complex web of allegiances and adapt to the changing authorities. The long-term effects of these multiple occupations on the political landscape were profound, shaping the post-war era and the rebuilding of Warsaw.

Today, Warsaw stands as a testament to the resilience of its people. The scars of war are still visible, but the city has risen from the ruins, rebuilding itself as a vibrant and thriving metropolis. Its history serves as a reminder of the indomitable spirit of those who endured the horrors of war.

In conclusion, Warsaw's journey from glory to ruins during World War II reflects the broader struggles faced by cities and countries in Eastern Europe. The impact of multiple occupations on major European cities was profound, affecting every aspect of life for the local population. Through the lens of Warsaw, we gain insight into the challenges faced by civilians, the role of resistance movements, the economic consequences, and the long-term effects on the political landscape. It is a story that deserves to be remembered and studied by historians, educators, students, and the public alike.

Berlin: The Epicenter of Power

During World War II, Berlin emerged as one of the most significant cities in Europe, serving as the epicenter of power and a key battleground for various factions. As a result, the German capital witnessed multiple occupations and experienced the far-reaching consequences of frequent changes in ownership.

Under several flags, Berlin endured numerous transformations that had a lasting impact on its inhabitants and the political landscape of the post-war era. The city's strategic importance as a hub of political, economic, and cultural influence made it a prime target for both the Allied and Axis powers.

With its central location, Berlin became a hotly contested territory, changing hands several times throughout the war. The military strategies employed by different factions to gain control of the city varied, ranging from large-scale offensives to urban warfare. The Battle of Berlin, fought in April and May 1945, marked the final stages of the war and saw intense street fighting and the eventual capture of the city by Soviet forces.

The impact of these multiple occupations on Berlin and its population was profound. Civilians faced immense challenges as they navigated life under different regimes, adapting to new laws, ideologies, and restrictions imposed by each occupying force. The cultural and social fabric of the city was significantly altered, as Berliners witnessed the destruction of landmarks, the displacement of communities, and the suppression of cultural expression.

Furthermore, the economic consequences of frequent changes in ownership took a toll on Berlin. The city's infrastructure was severely damaged, hindering post-war reconstruction and leaving a legacy of economic struggle. The long-term effects of these occupations shaped the political landscape of Berlin and Germany as a whole, with the division of the city into East and West and the subsequent Cold War tensions.

Today, Berlin stands as a testament to the resilience of its population and the enduring impact of World War II. The scars left by multiple occupations are still visible in the city's architecture, memorials, and collective memory. Understanding the complex history of Berlin during this turbulent period provides valuable insights into the challenges faced by civilians living in areas that were frequently occupied and the lasting consequences of such experiences on both a local and global scale.

As historians, educators, students, and the public, it is crucial to explore and study lesser-known cities and regions, like Berlin, that bore the brunt of multiple occupations during World War II. By examining the military strategies, economic consequences, cultural and social impact, and long-term effects, we can gain a deeper understanding of the human experience during this tumultuous period and shed light on the complexities of war and its aftermath.

Prague: A City Divided

During World War II, Prague, the capital city of Czechoslovakia, experienced a tumultuous journey marked by multiple occupations and shifting allegiances. Situated in the heart of Europe, Prague became a strategic prize for the warring factions, resulting in a city divided and a population caught in the crossfire.

Prague's geographical location made it an attractive target for both the Axis and Allied powers. As the war unfolded, the city changed hands several times, with German forces occupying Prague in 1939, followed by the Soviet Red Army in 1945. These repeated occupations not only disrupted the lives of the local population but also had profound economic, social, and cultural consequences.

The impact of these occupations on Prague's residents was profound. The city's inhabitants faced immense challenges as they navigated life under different regimes. The German occupation brought strict control and repression, while the Soviet occupation brought its own set of hardships and restrictions. The resistance movements played a crucial role in providing hope and support to the local population, acting as a symbol of resistance against the occupiers.

The recurring occupations also left a lasting imprint on Prague's landscape. The city's infrastructure suffered extensive damage during the war, and the subsequent reconstructions reflected the political changes that occurred. Soviet-inspired architecture and symbols replaced German influences, transforming the city's visual identity.

Economically, Prague faced severe consequences due to the frequent changes in ownership. The disruptions in trade and commerce, coupled with the destruction caused by the war, crippled the city's economy. The constant occupation hindered the development and stability of local industries, leaving a long-lasting impact on Prague's post-war recovery.

Moreover, the political landscape of Prague was forever altered by the multiple occupations. The shifting alliances and political ideologies shaped the city's post-war governance, leading to the establishment of a communist regime. The experiences of the war and subsequent occupations fueled political divisions and tensions that persisted for decades.

Prague's story is not unique, as many other cities and regions in Eastern Europe also experienced the turmoil of multiple occupations during World War II. The impact of these occupations on major European cities, the challenges faced by civilians, and the long-term consequences on political landscapes are crucial aspects of understanding the complexities of the war.

In conclusion, the story of Prague as a city divided during World War II sheds light on the broader narrative of Eastern Europe's turbulent journey through the war. Its recurring occupations illustrate the challenges faced by civilians, the economic consequences, and the lasting impact on the political and cultural landscape. Understanding the experiences of cities like Prague provides valuable insights into the complex history of World War II and its aftermath.

Lesser-known cities and regions that were heavily contested during World War II

In the grand narrative of World War II, there are certain cities and regions that have become synonymous with the conflict - Stalingrad, Berlin, and Normandy, to name a few. However, there are numerous lesser-known cities and regions that were also fiercely contested during this tumultuous period. These places, often overshadowed by their more famous counterparts, experienced the horrors of war and changed hands multiple times.

One such city is Lviv, located in modern-day Ukraine. Throughout the war, Lviv was under the control of four different powers - the Soviet Union, Nazi Germany, the Soviet Union again, and finally, Poland. This constant shifting of borders not only had a profound impact on the local population but also left the city scarred both physically and culturally. The successive occupations resulted in the destruction of historical landmarks and the displacement of thousands of residents.

Another lesser-known but heavily contested region was Białystok, also in modern-day Poland. This strategically important city changed hands several times between the Soviet Union and Nazi Germany during the early years of the war. The frequent occupation of Białystok had significant consequences for its inhabitants, who endured hardship and oppression under both regimes. The city's Jewish population, in particular, suffered greatly, with many being deported to concentration camps.

These lesser-known cities and regions were not only important strategically but also played a crucial role in the larger narrative of World War II. Key ports and harbors, such as the Latvian city of Liepāja, were repeatedly captured and recaptured by different factions. These ports served as vital supply lines and were hotly contested due to their strategic significance.

The recurring occupations of these cities and regions also gave rise to vibrant resistance movements. Local populations, weary of foreign rule, formed underground networks and fought back against their occupiers. These resistance movements, though often overshadowed by larger and more famous ones, played a crucial role in the overall resistance effort.

The economic consequences of repeated changes in ownership were also profound. Industries were disrupted, trade routes were disrupted, and the local economy suffered as a result. Civilians living in these frequently occupied areas faced numerous challenges, including scarcity of resources, food, and basic necessities.

The long-term effects of multiple occupations on the political landscape of these cities and regions cannot be underestimated. The post-war era saw a reshuffling of borders and the emergence of new nations. The scars of war and occupation continue to shape the cultural, social, and political fabric of these lesser-known cities and regions in Eastern Europe to this day.

In conclusion, while the major cities and battles of World War II often steal the spotlight, it is crucial to acknowledge the lesser-known cities and regions that were heavily contested during the conflict. These places experienced the horrors of war, changed hands multiple times, and endured the long-lasting consequences of frequent occupations. By examining their stories, we gain a deeper understanding of the wide-ranging impact of World War II on both the major cities and the lesser-known regions of Eastern Europe.

Lviv: A City Torn Apart

During World War II, Lviv, a city located in modern-day Ukraine, experienced a tumultuous journey as it changed hands multiple times between different factions. This subchapter delves into the intricate details of Lviv's history, shedding light on the impact of these recurring occupations on the city and its inhabitants.

Strategically positioned at the crossroads of Eastern Europe, Lviv became a coveted prize for the major powers involved in the war. As a result, the city witnessed fierce battles and constant shifting of control between the German forces, Soviet Union, and Polish resistance fighters.

The repeated occupations of Lviv had profound cultural, social, and economic consequences for its local population. The city's rich architectural heritage and its vibrant cultural identity suffered immense damage as each occupying force sought to exert control and impose their own ideologies. The residents of Lviv were subjected to different rules, languages, and cultural norms under each occupation, leading to a sense of identity crisis and a fragmented society.

The economic consequences of these frequent changes in ownership were also severe. The infrastructure of the city was heavily damaged, and the constant disruption hindered the functioning of businesses and industries. The local economy was thrown into chaos, exacerbating the hardships faced by the civilian population.

The resistance movements in Lviv played a crucial role in the city's struggle for freedom. Despite facing immense challenges, the Polish underground, Soviet partisans, and other resistance groups fought valiantly against the occupying forces. Their efforts not only hindered the enemy's progress but also provided hope and inspiration to the local population.

The challenges faced by civilians living in Lviv were immense. The constant threat of violence, the scarcity of basic necessities, and the fear of reprisals created an environment of constant anxiety and uncertainty. The residents had to adapt to the changing circumstances, often living under the control of different occupying forces within short periods of time.

The long-term effects of these multiple occupations were far-reaching, extending beyond the war itself. The political landscape of Lviv and the surrounding region underwent significant transformations as new boundaries were drawn and power dynamics shifted. The scars of World War II continued to shape the city's post-war era, influencing its political, social, and cultural development.

In conclusion, Lviv's experience during World War II exemplifies the challenges faced by cities and countries that changed hands multiple times. The impact of these recurring occupations on Lviv's cultural, social, and economic fabric was profound, leaving a lasting imprint on the city and its people. Understanding the history of cities like Lviv is crucial for historians, educators, students, and the public, as it provides valuable insights into the complexities and consequences of war.

Odessa: The Black Sea's Battleground

During World War II, the city of Odessa became one of the most fiercely contested territories in Eastern Europe. Situated on the shores of the Black Sea, its strategic location made it a highly coveted prize for both the Axis and Allied powers. The battles fought over this city had far-reaching impacts on both the local population and the broader geopolitical landscape.

Under several flags, Odessa changed hands multiple times throughout the war, enduring a series of brutal occupations. It was initially captured by Romanian forces in October 1941, who were part of the Axis powers. The Romanian occupiers imposed harsh rule over the local population, leading to widespread suffering and resistance.

However, the tide turned in 1944 when the Red Army launched a massive offensive to liberate the city. After months of fierce fighting, the Soviet forces emerged victorious and reclaimed Odessa from the Axis powers. The liberation marked a turning point in the war and dealt a significant blow to the Axis forces in the region.

The impact of these multiple occupations on Odessa and its people was profound. The city's infrastructure suffered extensive damage, with key ports and harbors being repeatedly captured and destroyed. The economic consequences were severe, as trade and commerce were disrupted, leaving the local population struggling to survive.

The cultural and social fabric of Odessa also underwent significant changes due to the recurring occupations. The local population experienced a mix of fear, uncertainty, and resilience as they witnessed the destruction of their city and the loss of loved ones. Resistance movements played a crucial role in providing hope and support to the people, organizing acts of sabotage and fostering a sense of unity among the occupied population.

The long-term effects of these multiple occupations were felt even after the war ended. The political landscape of Odessa and the surrounding region underwent significant transformations, as new governments were established and allegiances shifted. The scars of war remained visible for years, as the city struggled to rebuild and recover from the devastation.

Today, the story of Odessa serves as a reminder of the challenges faced by civilians living in areas that were frequently occupied during World War II. It highlights the resilience of the human spirit and the enduring impact of war on both individuals and communities. By studying the history of this city, we gain a deeper understanding of the complexities of war and the lasting consequences it can have on cities, countries, and their people.

Riga: A Flashpoint of Conflict

During World War II, the city of Riga became a major flashpoint of conflict in Eastern Europe. This subchapter delves into the turbulent journey experienced by Riga and its impact on the local population, economy, and political landscape.

Riga, the capital of Latvia, changed hands multiple times during the war, facing occupation by various factions. Its strategic location as a major port and harbor made it a coveted prize for both the Axis and the Allies. As such, Riga witnessed intense military strategies employed by different factions to gain control of the city.

The repeated occupations of Riga had far-reaching consequences for its inhabitants. The local population faced immense challenges as they were subjected to the whims of the occupying forces. Civilians had to adapt to changing political ideologies, cultural impositions, and social upheavals. The resistance movements in Riga played a crucial role in opposing the occupiers and providing support to the local population.

The economic consequences of frequent changes in ownership were also significant. The city's infrastructure suffered extensive damage, and the economy was severely disrupted. The continuous occupation hindered trade and development, affecting the livelihoods of the residents. The long-term effects of these economic disruptions would shape the post-war era for Riga.

The recurring occupations of Riga also had a profound impact on its cultural and social fabric. Local traditions and customs were suppressed or altered under different occupiers, leading to a loss of cultural identity for many. The population had to navigate the complexities of living under multiple ideologies, which often resulted in a fractured social landscape.

In the post-war era, Riga faced challenges in rebuilding and establishing a stable political landscape. The city's frequent changes in ownership complicated the process of establishing a unified government and determining its political trajectory. The long-lasting effects of multiple occupations continued to shape the political landscape of Riga and Latvia as a whole.

The story of Riga during World War II offers valuable insights into the experiences of cities and countries that changed hands multiple times. It highlights the struggles faced by civilians, the economic and cultural consequences, and the long-term effects on the political landscape. By understanding the complexities of Riga's journey, we gain a deeper understanding of the broader impact of World War II on Eastern Europe.

The strategic importance of key ports and harbors that were repeatedly captured during World War II

During World War II, several key ports and harbors in Eastern Europe played a crucial role in the military strategies employed by different factions. These ports, such as Odessa, Sevastopol, and Danzig, were repeatedly captured and recaptured by various armies, leaving a lasting impact on the region.

One of the main reasons for the strategic importance of these ports was their geographical location. Situated on major waterways, they provided access to vital trade routes and served as gateways to the rest of Europe. Controlling these ports meant controlling the flow of resources, troops, and supplies, giving the occupying army a significant advantage. Moreover, these ports also served as major naval bases, enabling the deployment of fleets and submarines, which could disrupt enemy shipping and support military operations.

The repeated capture of these key ports had significant consequences for the cities and countries involved. The impact on the local populations was immense, as civilians faced constant upheaval, destruction, and displacement. The cultural and social fabric of these cities and regions was deeply affected, as different occupying forces imposed their own ideologies and policies, leading to a clash of cultures and values. Resistance movements emerged in these areas, fighting against the occupiers and seeking to restore independence and freedom.

The economic consequences of frequent changes in ownership were also profound. The disruption of trade and commerce, coupled with the destruction of infrastructure, led to severe economic hardships for the local populations. The constant shifting of borders and the resulting political instability further hindered economic recovery, making it difficult for these cities and countries to rebuild in the post-war era.

Furthermore, the long-term effects of multiple occupations on the political landscape of these cities and countries cannot be ignored. The power struggles and rivalries that emerged during the war continued to shape the post-war political order. Governments were toppled, borders were redrawn, and new alliances were formed, all of which had lasting implications for the region.

Understanding the strategic importance of these key ports and harbors during World War II is essential for historians, educators, students, and the general public. By examining the military strategies employed, the challenges faced by civilians, and the long-term effects on the political and economic landscape, we can gain a deeper understanding of the complexities and consequences of the war. Only through this understanding can we truly appreciate the resilience and sacrifices of those who lived through this turbulent period in Eastern Europe's history.

Danzig/Gdansk: Gateway to the Baltic Sea

Located on the Baltic Sea, the city of Danzig, also known as Gdansk, holds a significant place in the history of Eastern Europe during World War II. This subchapter explores the city's role as a gateway to the Baltic Sea and the impact of multiple occupations on its population and landscape.

Danzig/Gdansk was a city that changed hands several times during World War II, making it a prime example for understanding the challenges faced by cities and countries in Eastern Europe that experienced frequent occupation. Its strategic location made it a coveted prize for different factions throughout the war.

The repeated capturing and recapturing of Danzig/Gdansk had profound consequences on its residents. The local population endured the hardships of war, living under different governing powers and facing economic instability. The occupation brought cultural and social upheaval, as the city's identity shifted with each change in ownership. Resistance movements played a crucial role in challenging the occupation forces and maintaining a sense of resilience among the local population.

The economic consequences of frequent changes in ownership were significant. The city's infrastructure suffered extensive damage, affecting its trade and industrial capacity. The long-term effects of these changes in ownership had a lasting impact on the political landscape of Danzig/Gdansk and the wider region.

Moreover, Danzig/Gdansk was not alone in experiencing such turbulence during World War II. Many lesser-known cities and regions in Eastern Europe were heavily contested, often serving as key ports and harbors. These strategic locations became magnets for military operations, as controlling them provided access to vital supply routes.

Understanding the military strategies employed by different factions to gain control of cities and countries during World War II is crucial to comprehending the complexity of the war. The challenges faced by civilians living in areas that were frequently occupied offer valuable insights into the human experience during this tumultuous period.

As historians, educators, students, and the general public, it is essential to study the impact of multiple occupations on major European cities. By examining the cultural, social, economic, and political consequences, we gain a deeper understanding of the long-term effects of World War II on the regions affected. Danzig/Gdansk serves as a compelling case study, shedding light on the struggles, resilience, and transformations experienced by cities and countries under several flags.

Sevastopol: The Naval Stronghold

Sevastopol, a city situated on the Crimean Peninsula, played a pivotal role as a naval stronghold during World War II. This subchapter explores the strategic importance of Sevastopol, its numerous occupations, and the impact of these recurring occupations on the city and its inhabitants.

With its deep-water harbor and proximity to the Black Sea, Sevastopol became a coveted prize for both the Axis and Allied powers. Its location made it a crucial hub for naval operations, allowing control over vital supply lines and the ability to project power across the region. As a result, Sevastopol witnessed intense fighting and changed hands multiple times during the war.

The German forces launched a major assault on Sevastopol in 1941, seeking to capture the city and gain control of the Black Sea. The Soviet defenders, however, valiantly resisted the German onslaught for nearly a year, inflicting heavy casualties and delaying the Axis advance. Eventually, the German forces emerged victorious, and Sevastopol fell under their control.

The occupation of Sevastopol by the Axis powers had profound consequences for the city and its population. The local inhabitants endured immense hardship, with severe restrictions on their daily lives and the imposition of a repressive regime. Yet, despite these challenges, resistance movements emerged, clandestinely working to undermine the occupiers and support the Allied cause.

In 1944, the tide of the war turned, and the Soviet forces launched a counteroffensive to reclaim Sevastopol. After months of intense fighting, the city was liberated, marking a significant turning point in the Eastern Front and dealing a severe blow to the German forces.

The recurring occupations took a heavy toll on Sevastopol's infrastructure, economy, and cultural heritage. The city's once-thriving port suffered significant damage, hindering post-war recovery efforts. Moreover, the frequent changes in ownership disrupted the lives of civilians, causing displacement, loss of livelihood, and social upheaval.

The impact of the Sevastopol's multiple occupations extended beyond the war years. The city's political landscape underwent profound transformations, with the post-war era witnessing shifts in power and influence. Moreover, the long-lasting effects of the war and occupations continue to shape the region and its people to this day.

In conclusion, Sevastopol's role as a naval stronghold during World War II, its repeated occupations, and the lasting consequences of these events highlight the challenges faced by cities and countries that changed hands multiple times. The story of Sevastopol serves as a powerful testament to the resilience of its inhabitants and the enduring impact of war on both a local and global scale.

Constanța: A Prize in the Black Sea

During World War II, the city of Constanța, located on the shores of the Black Sea, became a highly contested and strategically important location. This subchapter explores the significance of Constanța and its experiences as a city that changed hands multiple times during the war.

Constanța was a coveted prize for several reasons. Firstly, it served as a major port and harbor, making it a crucial logistical hub for the Axis and Allied powers. Its strategic location allowed for the transportation of troops, supplies, and resources to be efficiently carried out. Secondly, the city was home to valuable oil refineries, which were essential for the war effort. Controlling Constanța meant gaining access to these vital resources.

The repeated occupations of Constanța had a profound impact on the local population. Civilians faced numerous challenges as they endured the hardships of war and the constant presence of different factions. The social and cultural fabric of the city was deeply affected, as residents had to adapt to changing circumstances and ideologies imposed by new occupiers. Resistance movements played a crucial role in Constanţa, with locals organizing underground networks to sabotage enemy operations and provide support to their own forces.

The economic consequences of Constanţa's frequent changes in ownership were significant. The city's infrastructure suffered extensive damage, and the disruptions to trade and commerce had long-lasting effects on the local economy. The post-war era saw Constanţa grappling with the task of rebuilding and recovering from the devastation of war.

From a broader perspective, Constanţa's experiences reflect the larger story of Eastern Europe during World War II. The region was a hotbed of conflict, with numerous cities and countries changing hands multiple times. The impact of these occupations on major European cities was immense, as they faced destruction, displacement, and a loss of identity.

Understanding the military strategies employed by different factions to gain control of cities like Constanţa provides valuable insights into the dynamics of the war. It also sheds light on the long-term effects of multiple occupations on the political landscape of cities and countries in the post-war era.

Constanţa's turbulent journey through World War II serves as a poignant reminder of the immense sacrifices made by civilians and the resilience they displayed in the face of adversity. By examining the experiences of this lesser-known city, we gain a deeper understanding of the challenges faced by those living in areas that were frequently occupied during the war.

The role of resistance movements in cities and countries that changed hands multiple times during World War II

Throughout the course of World War II, numerous cities and countries in Eastern Europe experienced the turmoil of changing hands multiple times. These areas were hotly contested by various factions, resulting in significant cultural, social, economic, and political upheaval. In the face of constant occupation, resistance movements emerged as a crucial force in these war-torn regions.

Resistance movements played a vital role in cities and countries that faced recurring occupations. These movements were comprised of courageous individuals who refused to accept the status quo and were determined to fight for their freedom. Operating underground, they engaged in acts of sabotage, espionage, and guerrilla warfare, effectively disrupting the occupiers' plans and weakening their control.

One of the key contributions of resistance movements was their ability to gather and disseminate intelligence. These networks of informants and spies provided crucial information about the occupiers' movements, strategies, and weaknesses. This intelligence not only helped resistance fighters plan effective attacks but also enabled them to protect civilians and minimize casualties.

Resistance movements also served as a beacon of hope for the local populations. In the midst of despair and uncertainty, these movements embodied the spirit of resistance and resilience. They provided a sense of unity and purpose, rallying people together to resist the occupiers and reclaim their freedom. Through their acts of defiance and bravery, resistance fighters instilled a sense of pride and determination within their communities.

The impact of resistance movements extended beyond the military realm. They played a significant role in preserving cultural and social identities during the occupation. By actively resisting the occupiers' attempts to suppress local traditions, languages, and customs, resistance movements played a crucial role in maintaining a sense of identity and cohesion amongst the local population.

Additionally, resistance movements were instrumental in preparing for the post-war era. These movements often laid the groundwork for future political organizations and governments. Many resistance fighters went on to become influential leaders and decision-makers, shaping the political landscape of their cities and countries in the aftermath of the war.

The role of resistance movements in cities and countries that changed hands multiple times during World War II cannot be overstated. They were the driving force behind the resistance against occupiers, providing hope, protection, and a vision for a better future. Their contributions not only impacted the outcome of the war but also had significant long-term effects on the political, social, and cultural landscapes of these regions.

Warsaw Uprising: Defiance in the Face of Adversity

Amidst the chaos and turmoil of World War II, the city of Warsaw became a symbol of courage and defiance in the face of adversity. The Warsaw Uprising, a heroic act of resistance against the German occupation, stands as a testament to the indomitable spirit of the Polish people and the lengths they were willing to go to reclaim their city.

In the subchapter titled "Warsaw Uprising: Defiance in the Face of Adversity," we delve into the captivating story of this historic event, shedding light on the strategic importance of Warsaw and the challenges faced by its inhabitants during multiple occupations. Historians, educators, students, and the public will gain a comprehensive understanding of the impact of recurring occupations on major European cities during World War II.

We explore the military strategies employed by different factions to gain control of Warsaw, as well as the economic and political consequences of frequent changes in ownership. Through a careful examination of the resistance movements that sprouted within the city, we highlight the role of ordinary citizens turned heroes, their acts of sabotage, and their unwavering determination to liberate their homeland.

Furthermore, we analyze the cultural and social impact of recurring occupations on the local population, shedding light on the resilience and adaptability of the people of Warsaw. We delve into the long-term effects of multiple occupations on the political landscape of the city and the country, revealing the lasting scars and the challenges faced during the post-war era.

This subchapter will resonate with historians, educators, students, and the public interested in the impact of multiple occupations on major European cities during World War II. It will also captivate those intrigued by the lesser-known cities and regions that were heavily contested during the war. Additionally, it will provide valuable insights for those exploring the economic consequences of frequent changes in ownership and the challenges faced by civilians living in areas that were frequently occupied.

The story of the Warsaw Uprising is one of defiance, sacrifice, and resilience. By understanding the struggles and triumphs of those who fought for their city, we gain a deeper appreciation for the human spirit and the extraordinary lengths people will go to protect their homes and freedoms.

Partisans of the Forest: Guerrilla Warfare in Eastern Europe

Throughout World War II, Eastern Europe witnessed a tumultuous journey as cities and countries changed hands multiple times. Amidst this chaos, one group emerged as a symbol of resistance and resilience – the partisans of the forest. Engaging in guerrilla warfare, these brave individuals fought against occupying forces, leaving an indelible mark on the region's history.

The forests of Eastern Europe became the battleground and sanctuary for these partisans. Operating in small, mobile units, they struck at the heart of the occupiers' operations, disrupting supply lines, ambushing convoys, and sabotaging infrastructure. Their tactics, rooted in their deep knowledge of the terrain, allowed them to wage a clandestine war against the enemy.

Under several flags, cities and countries in Eastern Europe faced the wrath of multiple occupations during World War II. From Warsaw to Belgrade, Budapest to Bucharest, these urban centers became the epicenter of power struggles and conflicts. The partisans of the forest played a vital role in safeguarding their homelands and protecting their fellow citizens from the horrors of occupation.

The impact of these recurring occupations on major European cities was profound. The constant shift in power led to a fractured social fabric, as civilians faced the challenges of living under different regimes. The economic consequences were dire, as resources were plundered and infrastructure destroyed. The cultural and social fabric of these cities bore the scars of war, affecting generations to come.

Under the strategic importance of key ports and harbors, they were repeatedly captured and recaptured during the war. The resistance movements played a crucial role in disrupting enemy control and safeguarding these vital lifelines. The challenges faced by civilians living in these areas were immense, as they navigated the ever-changing political landscape and endured the hardships of occupation.

The long-term effects of these multiple occupations on the political landscape cannot be understated. The experiences of resistance and resilience shaped the post-war era, as countries and cities rebuilt themselves from the ashes. The partisans of the forest left a lasting legacy, reminding the world of the power of ordinary individuals in the face of adversity.

In "Shifting Borders: Eastern Europe's Turbulent Journey through World War II," we delve deep into the stories of these remarkable individuals and their impact on Eastern Europe's history. This subchapter sheds light on the critical role played by the partisans of the forest, offering an in-depth analysis of their military strategies, the challenges faced by civilians, and the far-reaching consequences of their actions. By exploring the cultural, social, economic, and political dimensions, we aim to provide a comprehensive understanding of the complex dynamics that shaped Eastern Europe during this turbulent period.

This subchapter will captivate historians, educators, students, and the wider public who seek to uncover the hidden stories of resistance and resilience amidst the chaos of World War II. It will particularly appeal to those interested in the impact of multiple occupations on major European cities, the challenges faced by civilians, and the long-term effects on the political landscape of the post-war era. Join us on this journey to discover the untold tales of the partisans of the forest and their indomitable spirit.

The Battle of Narva: Estonian Resistance

During World War II, the Eastern European region witnessed numerous cities and countries changing hands multiple times. These shifting borders resulted in significant challenges for the local populations, both economically and socially. One such city that experienced the brunt of these frequent changes was Narva, a strategically important city located on the border between Estonia and Russia.

The Battle of Narva, which took place between 1941 and 1944, was a pivotal event in the resistance efforts of the Estonian people against the occupying forces. The city had already been occupied by the Soviet Union in 1940, but in 1941, when the Germans launched their offensive against the Soviet Union, Narva became a major battleground.

The Estonian resistance movement played a crucial role in the Battle of Narva. Despite being caught between two occupying forces, many Estonians were determined to fight for their independence. They formed underground resistance groups and engaged in acts of sabotage against both the Soviet and German forces. The resistance fighters were not only Estonians but also included individuals from other Baltic countries who shared the same goal of liberating their homelands.

The Battle of Narva was marked by intense fighting, with both sides employing various military strategies to gain control of the city. The Germans, aware of the strategic importance of Narva's ports and harbors, launched several offensives to capture the city from the Soviets. On the other hand, the Soviets were equally determined to hold onto the city as part of their defensive strategy.

The frequent changes in ownership had a profound impact on the local population. Civilians living in Narva faced numerous challenges, including economic instability, as the city's resources were constantly depleted by the occupying forces. The cultural and social fabric of the city also suffered, as different factions imposed their ideologies on the local population.

After years of intense fighting, the Battle of Narva finally came to an end in 1944, when the Soviet Union managed to regain control of the city. However, the long-term effects of the multiple occupations were far-reaching. The political landscape of Narva, as well as the entire region, underwent significant changes in the post-war era.

The Battle of Narva serves as a testament to the resilience and determination of the Estonian people in the face of adversity. It also sheds light on the challenges faced by civilians living in areas that were frequently occupied during World War II. By studying the history of cities and countries that changed hands multiple times, we gain a deeper understanding of the impact of war on both individuals and societies, helping us to build a more informed and compassionate future.

The cultural and social impact of recurring occupations on local populations during World War II

During World War II, many cities and countries in Eastern Europe experienced multiple occupations by different factions. These recurring occupations had a profound cultural and social impact on the local populations, shaping their identities and leaving lasting scars on their communities.

One of the major consequences of these recurring occupations was the disruption of daily life for civilians. Families were torn apart, homes were destroyed, and communities were fractured. The constant fear and uncertainty of living under occupation took a toll on the mental and emotional well-being of the local populations. The occupying forces often imposed strict rules and regulations, suppressing local customs, traditions, and languages. The local populations were forced to adapt to the cultural norms and values of the occupiers, leading to a loss of their own cultural heritage.

Resistance movements played a crucial role in cities and countries that changed hands multiple times during the war. These movements, comprised of brave individuals who risked their lives, fought against the occupying forces and preserved their cultural identity. Through acts of sabotage, underground publications, and secret gatherings, they kept the flame of resistance alive. The resistance movements became symbols of hope and resilience for the local populations, inspiring them to hold on to their cultural heritage.

The economic consequences of frequent changes in ownership were devastating for the local populations. Industries were destroyed, infrastructure was damaged, and resources were depleted. The constant shifting of borders disrupted trade and commerce, leading to economic instability and poverty. The local populations had to endure rationing, scarcity, and a decline in their standard of living.

The long-term effects of multiple occupations on the political landscape were significant. The post-war era saw the emergence of new political ideologies and power struggles. The divisions caused by the recurring occupations were exploited by different factions, leading to political instability and social unrest. The scars of the war continue to shape the political landscape of these cities and countries even today.

In conclusion, the cultural and social impact of recurring occupations during World War II on local populations in Eastern Europe cannot be underestimated. The disruptions to daily life, the suppression of cultural identity, and the economic consequences continue to reverberate through these communities. Understanding these impacts is crucial for historians, educators, students, and the public to comprehend the full extent of the human experience during this turbulent period in history.

Cultural Suppression: The Struggle for Identity

During World War II, the cities and countries of Eastern Europe experienced a turbulent journey, changing hands multiple times. This subchapter, titled "Cultural Suppression: The Struggle for Identity," explores the profound impact of recurring occupations on the local populations and the long-term consequences it had on the political landscape of these regions.

The repeated occupations of cities and countries had far-reaching effects on the cultural and social fabric of Eastern Europe. Local populations were subjected to various forms of cultural suppression, as the occupiers sought to impose their own ideologies and erase the indigenous identity. Historians and educators will delve into the struggles faced by civilians living in these areas, exploring the challenges they encountered in preserving their heritage and maintaining a sense of identity amid the chaos of war.

The book will shed light on the lesser-known cities and regions that were heavily contested during World War II. It will examine the strategic importance of key ports and harbors that were repeatedly captured, providing insights into the military strategies employed by different factions to gain control. Through this, historians and students will gain a comprehensive understanding of the complex geopolitical landscape of Eastern Europe during this period.

A significant focus will be placed on the role of resistance movements in cities and countries that changed hands multiple times. These movements played a pivotal role in safeguarding local culture and identity, and their stories deserve recognition. By examining their efforts and sacrifices, the book aims to honor their contributions and inspire future generations.

Furthermore, this subchapter will explore the economic consequences of frequent changes in ownership. The constant disruptions hindered the development of stable economies, leaving lasting scars on the affected regions. Understanding these economic challenges is crucial in comprehending the post-war era and its effects on the political landscape.

Addressed to historians, educators, students, and the wider public, "Shifting Borders: Eastern Europe's Turbulent Journey through World War II" offers a unique perspective on the impact of multiple occupations. By delving into the struggles faced by local populations, it provides a comprehensive account of the cultural, social, economic, and political repercussions of recurring occupations. Through this exploration, the book aims to shed light on a lesser-known aspect of World War II history and foster a deeper understanding of the complex forces at play in Eastern Europe during this tumultuous era.

Social Fragmentation: Divisions and Collaboration

During World War II, Eastern Europe experienced a turbulent journey, with cities and countries often changing hands multiple times. This subchapter explores the social fragmentation that occurred as a result of these divisions, as well as the unexpected collaborations that emerged amidst the chaos. It sheds light on the lesser-known cities and regions heavily contested during the war and examines the impact of recurring occupations on the local populations.

The strategic importance of key ports and harbors that were repeatedly captured cannot be overstated. These locations served as vital supply routes and military bases, making them hotly contested throughout the war. The constant changes in ownership had significant economic consequences, as trade and commerce were disrupted, and infrastructure was destroyed in the process.

The military strategies employed by different factions to gain control of these cities and countries varied, but the resistance movements played a crucial role. The local populations, often faced with the challenges of living in areas frequently occupied, organized themselves into underground resistance movements. These groups fought against the occupiers, both for their own freedom and to support the larger allied cause.

The impact of multiple occupations went beyond the physical damage and economic repercussions. The recurring divisions led to social fragmentation, with communities torn apart by conflicting loyalties and ideologies. Families were separated, friendships strained, and mistrust permeated daily life. The cultural and social fabric of these regions underwent significant changes as different occupying forces imposed their own rules and values.

As the war drew to a close, the long-term effects of multiple occupations became apparent in the post-war era. The political landscape of cities and countries in Eastern Europe was transformed, with new borders and ideologies taking hold. The scars of social fragmentation and collaboration endured, shaping the collective memory and identity of these regions for decades to come.

This subchapter delves into the complex dynamics of social fragmentation and collaboration during World War II in Eastern Europe. By examining the experiences of civilians, the military strategies employed, and the long-term consequences, it offers a comprehensive understanding of the challenges faced by these communities. Historians, educators, students, and the public will gain valuable insights into the lesser-known aspects of this tumultuous period in history.

The Displaced: Refugees and Dislocation

During World War II, the Eastern European region witnessed a turbulent journey as cities and countries changed hands multiple times. This subchapter, titled "The Displaced: Refugees and Dislocation," explores the profound impact of these frequent occupations on major European cities, lesser-known regions, and the lives of local populations.

One of the key aspects that emerged from this period was the displacement of millions of people. As cities and countries fell under different flags, civilians found themselves uprooted from their homes, forced to flee in search of safety. The scale of this displacement was unprecedented, and its consequences are still felt today. Through firsthand accounts and historical records, this subchapter sheds light on the challenges faced by these refugees, their struggles to find shelter, and the efforts made by organizations and individuals to aid them.

Furthermore, this subchapter delves into the cultural and social impact of recurring occupations. The constant flux of power led to the suppression and erasure of local identities, as occupying forces imposed their own ideologies and values. The resilience of resistance movements in these cities and countries becomes a focal point of analysis, as they fought to preserve their cultural heritage and resist foreign domination.

The economic consequences of frequent changes in ownership are also examined. The constant disruption of trade routes, the destruction of infrastructure, and the pillaging of resources had a detrimental effect on the local economies. This subchapter explores the long-lasting repercussions of these economic disruptions and the challenges faced by civilians in rebuilding their lives and livelihoods.

From a military perspective, the subchapter discusses the strategies employed by different factions to gain control of cities and countries. It analyzes the significance of key ports and harbors that were repeatedly captured, highlighting their strategic importance in the larger context of the war.

Finally, this subchapter investigates the long-term effects of multiple occupations on the political landscape of cities and countries in the post-war era. It examines how these recurring occupations shaped the political ideologies, alliances, and power dynamics in the region, ultimately leaving a lasting impact on the geopolitical landscape of Eastern Europe.

"The Displaced: Refugees and Dislocation" offers historians, educators, students, and the general public a comprehensive understanding of the consequences of frequent occupations during World War II. By exploring the experiences of individuals, the subchapter provides nuanced insights into the challenges, resilience, and transformations that shaped the lives of those living in cities and regions that changed hands multiple times.

The economic consequences of frequent changes in ownership during World War II

During World War II, many cities and countries in Eastern Europe experienced multiple changes in ownership, as different factions fought for control over strategic locations. These frequent changes in ownership had significant economic consequences for the affected regions.

One of the major economic consequences was the disruption of trade and commerce. As ownership changed hands, trade routes were disrupted, and businesses were forced to halt their operations or adapt to new owners and regulations. This led to a decline in economic activity and a loss of income for many local populations.

Additionally, the constant changes in ownership resulted in the destruction of infrastructure and industrial facilities. Bombings and military operations often targeted key economic centers, leaving cities and regions in ruins. This not only caused immediate economic setbacks but also hindered the post-war reconstruction efforts.

The fluctuating ownership also led to the displacement of populations. Many people were forced to flee their homes and seek refuge in other areas, disrupting communities and eroding social networks. This mass migration further strained local economies and created a refugee crisis.

Furthermore, the frequent changes in ownership during World War II resulted in the looting and pillaging of resources. Both occupying forces and retreating armies often seized valuable assets, including food, machinery, and raw materials. This plundering depleted local resources and hindered economic recovery.

The economic consequences were not limited to immediate wartime effects. The constant changes in ownership also had long-term implications for the post-war era. The destruction of infrastructure, loss of skilled labor, and disruption of trade routes hindered the economic development of the affected regions for years to come. The political landscape was also reshaped, with new governments often implementing different economic policies, further complicating the recovery process.

In conclusion, the frequent changes in ownership during World War II had severe economic consequences for cities and countries in Eastern Europe. Disrupted trade, destroyed infrastructure, displacement of populations, resource plundering, and long-term economic setbacks were some of the major challenges faced by these regions. Understanding the economic impact of recurring occupations during World War II is crucial for historians, educators, students, and the general public to grasp the full extent of the war's consequences on Eastern Europe's turbulent journey.

Pillaging and Plundering: Economic Exploitation

During World War II, the cities and countries of Eastern Europe became the epicenter of a fierce struggle for power and control. Countless regions changed hands multiple times, leaving a trail of destruction, suffering, and economic exploitation in their wake. In this subchapter, we will delve into the economic consequences of frequent changes in ownership and the impact they had on the local populations.

The recurring occupations of cities and countries during World War II brought about a wave of economic exploitation. Invading forces often engaged in pillaging and plundering, stripping these areas of their valuable resources. Artifacts, artworks, and treasures were looted, while industries and factories were dismantled and transported to the conqueror's homeland for their economic benefit.

Major European cities that changed hands frequently, such as Warsaw, Berlin, and Budapest, suffered immense economic losses. The constant destruction and rebuilding efforts drained the resources of these cities, leaving them in a state of economic ruin. Similarly, lesser-known cities and regions that were heavily contested, like Lviv and Danzig, experienced significant economic setbacks as they struggled to recover from the constant disruptions.

Key ports and harbors played a crucial role in the war efforts, and their strategic importance made them prime targets for multiple occupations. The repeated capture of these ports led to disruptions in trade and commerce, causing severe economic hardships for the local populations. The constant changes in ownership hindered the flow of goods and services, leaving civilians grappling with shortages and inflation.

Resistance movements emerged in response to the frequent occupations, striving to protect their cities and countries from economic exploitation. These movements played a vital role in sabotaging the invaders' efforts to exploit local resources. They carried out acts of resistance, such as smuggling and sabotage, to disrupt the economic activities of the occupiers.

The economic consequences of frequent changes in ownership had long-term effects on the political landscape of Eastern Europe in the post-war era. The economic exploitation perpetuated by the occupiers fueled resentment and shaped the post-war political agenda. It laid the groundwork for the rise of nationalist movements and the push for independence in many Eastern European countries.

In conclusion, the economic exploitation resulting from the pillaging and plundering during World War II had a profound impact on the cities and countries of Eastern Europe. The constant changes in ownership, the destruction of industries, the disruption of trade, and the depletion of resources all contributed to immense economic hardships for the local populations. Understanding the economic consequences of these frequent occupations sheds light on the challenges faced by civilians and the long-term effects on the political and economic landscape of the region.

Industrial Destruction: Infrastructure in Ruins

During World War II, Eastern Europe experienced a turbulent journey as cities and countries changed hands multiple times. This subchapter, titled "Industrial Destruction: Infrastructure in Ruins," delves into the profound impact of these frequent occupations on the region's infrastructure and economy.

The strategic importance of key ports and harbors became apparent as they were repeatedly captured by different factions. These vital transportation hubs, such as Gdansk and Odessa, endured significant damage. The military strategies employed to gain control of these cities often resulted in heavy bombardments and destruction, leaving the infrastructure in ruins.

Not only were key ports affected, but lesser-known cities and regions also became heavily contested battlegrounds. Places like Lviv, Minsk, and Königsberg found themselves caught in the crossfire, suffering immense damage. The destruction of factories, railways, and bridges crippled the industrial capabilities of these areas, exacerbating the economic consequences of the war.

The impact on local populations cannot be overlooked. Civilians living in areas that were frequently occupied faced numerous challenges. They endured constant displacement, destruction of their homes, and the disruption of essential services. Resistance movements emerged as a vital force in these cities and countries, striving to protect their communities and infrastructure from further devastation.

Beyond the immediate effects, the long-term consequences of multiple occupations shaped the political landscape in the post-war era. The recurring occupations left deep scars on the region, fostering ethnic tensions and political divisions that persist to this day. The cultural and social impact on local populations was profound, as they struggled to rebuild their lives amidst the ruins of war.

This subchapter sheds light on the often-overlooked economic consequences of frequent changes in ownership. The destruction of factories and infrastructure disrupted production and trade, setting back regional economies for years. The post-war era witnessed a slow and arduous process of reconstruction, as cities and countries worked to rebuild their industries and restore their economies.

"Industrial Destruction: Infrastructure in Ruins" offers an in-depth exploration of the challenges faced by Eastern Europe during World War II. It provides valuable insights for historians, educators, students, and the public, shedding light on the lesser-known cities and regions that were heavily contested. By understanding the economic, cultural, and social impacts of recurring occupations, we gain a deeper appreciation for the lasting legacy of this turbulent period in history.

The Shadow of Inflation: Currency Instability

During World War II, the Eastern European region experienced a series of rapid and frequent changes in ownership of cities and countries. These constant shifts in power had profound effects on various aspects of life, including the economy. One of the major challenges faced by the local populations was the shadow of inflation and currency instability.

As different factions gained control over cities and countries, they often introduced their own currency or manipulated existing ones to suit their needs. This resulted in a chaotic and unstable economic environment, where the value of money fluctuated wildly, and inflation soared to unprecedented levels.

The impact of currency instability was felt by both the local populations and the occupying forces. For the civilians, it meant a constant struggle to meet their basic needs. Prices skyrocketed, making everyday goods and services unaffordable for many. People had to resort to bartering or relying on the black market to survive.

The occupying forces also faced significant challenges due to currency instability. They had to deal with a devalued currency, which made it difficult for them to maintain their military operations and supply lines. The constant changes in currency also complicated their efforts to control and stabilize the occupied territories.

The economic consequences of currency instability were far-reaching. Inflation eroded the savings and wealth of the local populations, leading to widespread poverty and economic hardship. It also undermined the stability of the market, affecting trade and investment. The lack of a stable currency hindered economic growth and development, leaving a lasting impact on the post-war era.

Currency instability was not only a result of frequent changes in ownership but also a deliberate strategy employed by different factions to weaken their opponents. By manipulating the currency, they sought to undermine the economic stability of the occupied territories and gain an upper hand in the conflict.

In conclusion, the shadow of inflation and currency instability loomed large over Eastern Europe during World War II. The constant changes in ownership and the manipulation of currencies had devastating effects on the economy and the lives of the local populations. Understanding the economic consequences of frequent changes in ownership is crucial for historians, educators, students, and the general public to comprehend the full impact of World War II on Eastern Europe.

The military strategies employed by different factions to gain control of cities and countries during World War II

The military strategies employed by different factions to gain control of cities and countries during World War II were diverse and complex. As the war raged on, various factions such as the Axis powers (Germany, Italy, and Japan) and the Allied forces (United States, Soviet Union, and their allies) employed different tactics to secure control over key territories.

One of the main strategies employed was the use of blitzkrieg or "lightning war" tactics. This involved swift and coordinated attacks using combined arms, including tanks, aircraft, and infantry. The German forces, in particular, utilized this strategy to great effect, quickly overwhelming their opponents and capturing cities and countries. Their success relied on the element of surprise, rapid movement, and the exploitation of weak points in the enemy's defenses.

Another crucial strategy was the use of amphibious assaults to capture key ports and harbors. The Allied forces, led by the United States and the United Kingdom, employed this tactic in several crucial operations, such as the D-Day invasion of Normandy. By capturing strategic ports, they were able to establish supply lines and launch subsequent offensives into enemy territory.

Resistance movements also played a significant role in gaining control of cities and countries. In areas that were heavily contested, local populations organized themselves into partisan groups, engaging in guerrilla warfare against the occupying forces. These resistance movements disrupted enemy supply lines, gathered intelligence, and conducted sabotage operations, ultimately contributing to the liberation of their cities and countries.

The impact of these military strategies on the local populations was profound. Civilians living in areas that changed hands multiple times faced immense challenges, including bombings, forced labor, and displacement. The recurring occupations also had a significant cultural and social impact, as different factions imposed their ideologies and values on the local populations.

Furthermore, the economic consequences of frequent changes in ownership were staggering. Industries were disrupted, infrastructure was destroyed, and resources were depleted as cities and countries were repeatedly ravaged by warfare.

The long-term effects of multiple occupations on the political landscape were also substantial. The post-war era saw significant geopolitical changes, as borders were redrawn, new governments were established, and power dynamics shifted. Many cities and countries in Eastern Europe underwent radical transformations, as they transitioned from occupation to independence or incorporation into new political entities.

Overall, the military strategies employed during World War II to gain control of cities and countries were multifaceted and had far-reaching consequences. Understanding these strategies is essential for historians, educators, students, and the public to comprehend the complexities of this turbulent period in history and the lasting impact it had on the world.

Blitzkrieg: Germany's Lightning War

The Blitzkrieg, or "lightning war," was a revolutionary military strategy employed by Germany during World War II that had a profound impact on the cities and countries of Eastern Europe. This subchapter explores the strategic significance, military tactics, and long-term consequences of the Blitzkrieg on the region.

The Blitzkrieg was characterized by its unprecedented speed and coordination, as German forces rapidly advanced through Eastern Europe, capturing cities and territories in lightning-fast campaigns. This strategy aimed to utilize the element of surprise, overwhelming firepower, and swift movement to paralyze and disorient the enemy. The German forces, armed with tanks, aircraft, and mechanized infantry, broke through enemy lines, encircled opposing armies, and quickly neutralized resistance. The Blitzkrieg was a crucial factor in Germany's early success in the war, as it allowed them to swiftly conquer Poland, Denmark, Norway, the Low Countries, and France.

However, the Blitzkrieg also had significant consequences for the cities and countries caught in its path. Eastern European cities such as Warsaw, Rotterdam, and Paris became heavily contested battlegrounds, changing hands multiple times over the course of the war. This constant flux of ownership had profound effects on the local populations, who endured the destruction and chaos of repeated occupations. Civilians faced immense challenges, including displacement, shortages of food and resources, and the trauma of living under constant threat.

Resistance movements played a vital role in cities and countries that experienced multiple occupations. Underground networks, such as the Polish Home Army and the French Resistance, operated in secret, carrying out acts of sabotage, espionage, and guerrilla warfare against the occupying forces. These movements represented a symbol of hope and defiance for the local populations, and their actions contributed to the eventual liberation of many cities and territories.

The economic consequences of frequent changes in ownership were severe. Industries were disrupted, infrastructure was damaged, and resources were depleted. Furthermore, the cultural and social fabric of these cities and countries were profoundly affected. The occupiers sought to impose their own ideologies, suppress local cultures, and exploit resources for their own benefit.

The long-term effects of the Blitzkrieg and multiple occupations were also felt in the post-war era. Eastern Europe underwent significant political transformations as borders were redrawn and new governments were established. The scars of war and occupation continued to shape the political landscape, fostering deep-seated grievances and tensions that would persist for decades.

In conclusion, the Blitzkrieg was a military strategy that left an indelible mark on the cities and countries of Eastern Europe during World War II. Its lightning-fast campaigns and frequent changes in ownership had far-reaching consequences for the local populations, economies, and political landscapes. Understanding the impact of the Blitzkrieg provides valuable insights into the challenges faced by civilians, the strategies employed by factions, and the long-term legacies of World War II in Eastern Europe.

Soviet Steamroller: The Red Army's Advance

During World War II, the Soviet Red Army's advance across Eastern Europe was a pivotal and transformative event that shaped the course of the war and had long-lasting effects on the region. In this subchapter, we will delve into the Soviet steamroller and its impact on the cities and countries that changed hands multiple times during the war.

The Red Army's advance was marked by a series of relentless offensives that swept across Eastern Europe, pushing back German forces and liberating territories that had been occupied for years. Cities and regions such as Warsaw, Budapest, and Stalingrad became major battlegrounds, witnessing intense fighting and destruction. These places became symbols of resistance and resilience, as local populations faced the challenges of living in areas that were frequently occupied.

The strategic importance of key ports and harbors cannot be overstated. These locations were repeatedly captured and recaptured, as both the Axis and Allied forces recognized their significance in sustaining their war efforts. The constant tug-of-war for control over these ports disrupted trade and had significant economic consequences for the local populations.

Resistance movements played a crucial role in cities and countries that changed hands multiple times. Partisans and underground fighters engaged in sabotage, espionage, and guerrilla warfare, making it difficult for occupying forces to maintain control. These resistance movements not only disrupted enemy operations but also provided hope and inspiration to the local populations.

The cultural and social impact of recurring occupations was immense. Local populations experienced the trauma of war, witnessing the destruction of their homes, the loss of loved ones, and the displacement of communities. The repeated changes in ownership brought different ideologies, languages, and cultures to these areas, leaving a lasting impact on the post-war era.

The economic consequences of frequent changes in ownership were significant. Industries were disrupted, infrastructure was damaged, and economies were left in shambles. The rebuilding process after each occupation was a daunting task that required immense resources and effort.

The military strategies employed by different factions to gain control of cities and countries during the war varied. The Red Army utilized its vast numbers, combined with strategic planning and coordination, to overpower the enemy. Their advance was swift and relentless, often leaving a path of destruction in their wake.

The challenges faced by civilians living in areas that were frequently occupied cannot be understated. They endured hardships, scarcity of resources, and constant fear for their lives. The resilience and courage displayed by these individuals in the face of adversity is a testament to the human spirit.

In the post-war era, the long-term effects of multiple occupations shaped the political landscape of cities and countries. Borders were redrawn, governments were established, and new alliances were formed. The scars of war, both physical and psychological, remained as a constant reminder of the turbulent journey through World War II.

In conclusion, the Soviet steamroller's advance across Eastern Europe during World War II had a profound impact on the cities and countries that changed hands multiple times. The military strategies, economic consequences, and challenges faced by civilians shaped the region's history and had lasting effects on its political, social, and cultural landscape. Understanding this period is crucial in comprehending the complexities of Eastern Europe's journey through World War II and its aftermath.

Operation Barbarossa: Hitler's Eastern Front

Operation Barbarossa, launched on June 22, 1941, was Adolf Hitler's ambitious military campaign to conquer the Soviet Union and secure Germany's eastern front during World War II. This subchapter explores the various aspects of this significant operation and its profound impact on the cities and countries of Eastern Europe.

Under the codename Barbarossa, Hitler aimed to eradicate communism, acquire valuable resources, and create living space for the German people. However, this operation would prove to be a turning point in the war, as it encountered unexpected challenges and ultimately led to Germany's downfall.

Eastern Europe became a battleground for major European powers, with cities and countries changing hands multiple times during the war. This subchapter sheds light on the lesser-known cities and regions that were heavily contested, highlighting their strategic importance and the impact of frequent occupations on the local populations.

Resistance movements played a crucial role in these cities and countries, as they fought against the occupying forces and contributed to the eventual liberation. The subchapter delves into the strategies employed by different factions to gain control and the challenges faced by civilians living in areas that were frequently occupied.

The cultural, social, and economic consequences of recurring occupations cannot be overlooked. The subchapter explores how these occupations disrupted daily life, caused immense suffering, and left a lasting impact on the affected populations. It also examines the long-term effects on the political landscape of these cities and countries in the post-war era.

Furthermore, the subchapter explores the impact on key ports and harbors that were repeatedly captured during the war, affecting trade routes and military logistics. It also highlights the economic consequences of frequent changes in ownership and how these fluctuations disrupted trade and stability.

Addressed to historians, educators, students, and the public, this subchapter provides a comprehensive analysis of Operation Barbarossa and its implications. It aims to shed light on the often-overlooked regions and cities that experienced multiple occupations, examining the military strategies, resistance movements, and the long-term consequences of these turbulent times. By understanding this chapter of history, we can gain valuable insights into the challenges faced by civilians, the impact on culture and society, and the lasting effects on the political, economic, and social landscape of Eastern Europe.

The challenges faced by civilians living in areas that were frequently occupied during World War II

The challenges faced by civilians living in areas that were frequently occupied during World War II were immense and had a lasting impact on their lives. The constant change of ownership of cities and countries in Eastern Europe brought about a multitude of difficulties for the local populations.

One of the most significant challenges was the disruption of daily life. Civilians living in these areas had to constantly adapt to new rules and regulations imposed by different occupying powers. They had to navigate through a complex web of laws, restrictions, and curfews, which made it difficult for them to go about their everyday activities. Food shortages were also a common problem, as resources were often prioritized for the military or exported to the occupiers' home countries.

The recurring occupations also had a profound impact on the social fabric of these communities. Families were torn apart, with many men being conscripted into various armies and women left to fend for themselves. The constant fear and uncertainty led to a breakdown of trust among neighbors and communities. Collaboration and resistance movements emerged, further dividing the population and causing additional strife.

The economic consequences were also severe. The frequent changes in ownership disrupted trade and commerce, leaving many businesses bankrupt and people unemployed. Infrastructure, including roads, bridges, and buildings, was often destroyed or damaged during battles, further hampering the region's economy.

The psychological toll on the civilian population cannot be underestimated. Living under constant occupation, witnessing violence, and experiencing the loss of loved ones took a heavy toll on individuals and communities. Many suffered from trauma and post-war stress disorders, which often went unaddressed due to the lack of resources and support.

In the post-war era, the effects of these frequent occupations continued to shape the political landscape of the region. The divisions caused by collaboration and resistance movements, along with the lingering trauma and economic disparities, influenced the political ideologies and choices made by the people.

Understanding the challenges faced by civilians living in areas frequently occupied during World War II is crucial to comprehending the full impact of this turbulent period in history. It sheds light on the resilience of the human spirit, the complexities of war, and the long-lasting consequences that continue to shape Eastern Europe to this day.

Repression and Persecution: Life Under Oppression

In the tumultuous years of World War II, Eastern Europe bore witness to a relentless cycle of occupations and power shifts. Cities and countries in this region changed hands multiple times, leaving lasting scars on the lives of the people who lived under constant repression and persecution. This subchapter delves into the harrowing experiences of those who endured the hardships of life under oppression.

Throughout the war, lesser-known cities and regions in Eastern Europe found themselves heavily contested. These areas held strategic importance, as key ports and harbors were repeatedly captured by different factions. The military strategies employed by these factions were ruthless, and the challenges faced by civilians living in these areas were immense. The book explores the impact of these recurring occupations on the local populations, both culturally and socially.

Under constant threat, resistance movements emerged as a beacon of hope for the oppressed. Their heroic efforts to undermine the occupying forces and protect their communities are a testament to the resilience of the human spirit. By shedding light on the role of these resistance movements, the subchapter offers insight into the bravery and determination of those who fought against the forces of tyranny.

The economic consequences of frequent changes in ownership during the war were severe. The constant disruptions to trade and industry crippled the economies of these regions, leaving lasting scars on their development. Moreover, the long-term effects of multiple occupations on the political landscape of cities and countries in the post-war era were profound. The subchapter explores how the frequent changes in ownership shaped the political destiny of these regions, paving the way for new alliances and rivalries.

Addressing historians, educators, students, and the general public, this subchapter aims to shed light on the forgotten stories of those who lived under repression and persecution during World War II. By understanding the impact of multiple occupations on major European cities and the challenges faced by civilians, we gain a deeper appreciation for the resilience and courage displayed in the face of unimaginable adversity. Through this exploration, we gain a more comprehensive understanding of the complexities and consequences of war, and the lasting legacies it leaves behind.

Scarce Resources: Struggles for Survival

During World War II, the Eastern European region witnessed a tumultuous journey, as cities and countries changed hands multiple times. This subchapter explores the various struggles for survival faced by the local populations in these areas, highlighting the impact on both individuals and communities.

One of the key consequences of recurring occupations was the scarcity of resources. As different factions gained control, they often prioritized their own needs, leaving the local population to suffer. Basic necessities such as food, water, and shelter became scarce, forcing civilians to adapt and find innovative ways to survive. This scarcity also led to the rise of black markets and smuggling networks, as people sought to procure essential items.

The frequent changes in ownership also had a profound impact on major European cities. Urban centers such as Warsaw, Prague, and Budapest became hotly contested battlegrounds, resulting in extensive damage to infrastructure and loss of historical landmarks. The destruction of these cities not only had immediate consequences but also left a lasting impact on the cultural and social fabric of these regions.

Lesser-known cities and regions were also heavily contested during this period. Locations that were strategically important, such as key ports and harbors, were repeatedly captured by different factions. These areas became crucial for the transportation of troops, supplies, and weaponry, making them prime targets. The constant upheaval disrupted the lives of the local population and hindered economic development.

Resistance movements played a significant role in cities and countries that changed hands multiple times. These brave individuals and groups fought against the occupiers, both militarily and through acts of sabotage. Their efforts not only provided hope to the local population but also played a crucial role in weakening the occupying forces.

The economic consequences of frequent changes in ownership were severe. Industries were disrupted, trade routes were cut off, and many businesses were forced to shut down. The constant instability hindered economic growth and left a long-lasting impact on the post-war era.

Civilians living in areas that were frequently occupied faced numerous challenges. They had to navigate shifting allegiances, adapt to new laws and regulations, and endure the hardships brought on by war. The trauma and hardships experienced by these individuals left a lasting impact on their lives and the communities they belonged to.

In the post-war era, the political landscape of cities and countries that went through multiple occupations was significantly altered. The power dynamics shifted, new governments were established, and borders were redrawn. The scars of the past continued to shape the political trajectory of these regions for years to come.

In conclusion, the struggles for survival faced by the local populations in Eastern Europe during World War II were immense. Scarce resources, destruction of cities, resistance movements, economic consequences, and challenges faced by civilians all played a significant role in shaping the history and legacy of this turbulent period. Understanding these struggles provides valuable insights into the impact of war on individuals, communities, and nations.

Disrupted Lives: Constant Displacement

World War II was a period of unprecedented turmoil and upheaval in Eastern Europe, with cities and countries constantly changing hands between various factions. This subchapter delves into the profound impact of multiple occupations on major European cities, lesser-known regions, and the lives of the local populations. It explores the historical account of cities and countries that were caught under several flags during this tumultuous time, shedding light on the often overlooked consequences of frequent changes in ownership.

One of the key aspects examined in this subchapter is the strategic importance of key ports and harbors. These locations became hotly contested as different factions recognized their value in sustaining their military operations. The repeated capture and recapture of these ports not only disrupted trade and supply lines but also had lasting economic consequences for the regions.

Resistance movements played a crucial role in cities and countries that changed hands multiple times. These underground movements bravely fought against occupying forces, providing hope and inspiration to the local populations. The subchapter delves into the strategies employed by these resistance movements and their impact on the outcome of the war.

The cultural and social fabric of cities and regions also experienced profound changes due to recurring occupations. Local populations were subjected to the imposition of different ideologies and cultural practices, often leading to tensions and conflicts. The subchapter explores the long-lasting effects of these disruptions on the cultural identity of these areas.

Moreover, the economic consequences of frequent changes in ownership cannot be underestimated. The constant displacement of populations disrupted agriculture, industry, and trade, leaving a lasting impact on the economic landscape of these regions. The subchapter delves into the challenges faced by civilians living in areas that were frequently occupied, including scarcity of resources, displacement, and the constant threat of violence.

Finally, this subchapter examines the long-term effects of multiple occupations on the political landscape of cities and countries in the post-war era. The shifting borders and recurring occupations had a profound impact on the political dynamics of Eastern Europe, shaping the course of history for years to come.

"Disrupted Lives: Constant Displacement" offers a comprehensive exploration of the consequences of multiple occupations during World War II. It is a valuable resource for historians, educators, students, and the public, providing a deeper understanding of the challenges faced by those living in areas that were frequently occupied, and the lasting effects on the regions' political, social, and economic landscapes.

The long-term effects of multiple occupations on the political landscape of cities and countries in the post-war era

In the aftermath of World War II, many cities and countries in Eastern Europe experienced a turbulent journey, changing hands several times during the war. These recurring occupations had significant and lasting effects on the political landscape of these regions. Understanding these effects is crucial for historians, educators, students, and the general public, as it provides insights into the complexities and challenges faced by these areas during this period.

Cities and countries that changed hands multiple times during the war became sites of intense power struggles and political instability. The repeated transitions of ownership not only disrupted the lives of civilians but also had profound consequences for the development of political structures. The constant shifting of borders and allegiances created a fragmented political landscape, with competing factions vying for control.

The impact of multiple occupations on major European cities was particularly significant. These cities, such as Warsaw, Berlin, and Prague, became battlegrounds for opposing forces, resulting in extensive destruction and loss of life. The strategic importance of key ports and harbors that were repeatedly captured during the war further intensified the conflicts and added to the instability of these regions.

Resistance movements played a crucial role in cities and countries that changed hands multiple times. These movements, composed of courageous individuals who defied the occupiers, sought to preserve their national identity and resist oppressive regimes. Their actions not only inspired hope among the local populations but also had lasting effects on the post-war political landscape.

The cultural and social impact of recurring occupations on local populations cannot be overlooked. The imposition of different ideologies and values by occupiers often led to the erosion of cultural traditions and social norms. The economic consequences of frequent changes in ownership were also profound, as resources were exploited and infrastructure was damaged or destroyed.

The military strategies employed by different factions to gain control of cities and countries during the war had a lasting impact on the political landscape. These strategies shaped the power dynamics and influenced the post-war political systems, leading to the rise of new political parties and the marginalization of others.

Civilians living in areas that were frequently occupied faced immense challenges. They endured the hardships of war, including shortages of food, shelter, and basic necessities. Their lives were upended, and they often had to adapt to new political systems and ideologies imposed by each occupying force.

In the post-war era, the long-term effects of multiple occupations on the political landscape were evident. These effects included the redrawing of borders, the establishment of new governments, and the reconfiguration of power dynamics. The scars of the war and the recurring occupations continued to shape the political, social, and economic trajectory of these cities and countries for decades to come.

In conclusion, the long-term effects of multiple occupations on the political landscape of cities and countries in the post-war era were profound. Understanding these effects is crucial for historians, educators, students, and the public, as it provides insights into the challenges faced by these regions and sheds light on the complexities of this transformative period in history.

Power Shifts: Redrawing Borders

During World War II, Eastern Europe witnessed numerous power shifts and border redrawings that left a profound impact on cities and countries in the region. This subchapter delves into the complexities and consequences of these power shifts, addressing the historical, cultural, social, economic, and political aspects that emerged as a result.

Cities and countries in Eastern Europe became pawns in a relentless game of strategic importance during the war. From Warsaw to Stalingrad, these urban centers were repeatedly captured, occupied, and liberated by various factions. Their significance lay not only in their geographical location but also in their industrial capabilities, resources, and political influence.

Under Several Flags explores the lesser-known cities and regions that were heavily contested during the war. These often-overlooked areas faced the brunt of frequent occupations, resulting in immense challenges for the civilian population who had to endure not only the physical destruction of their homes but also the psychological trauma of living in a constant state of uncertainty and fear.

Resistance movements played a crucial role in cities and countries that changed hands multiple times. These underground networks operated clandestinely, sabotaging enemy operations, providing intelligence to allied forces, and fostering a sense of hope and resilience among the local populations.

The cultural and social impact of recurring occupations was profound. Local traditions, languages, and identities were suppressed and replaced with those of the occupying forces. The economic consequences were equally devastating, as industries were dismantled or repurposed to serve the occupiers' needs, leaving the local economies in shambles.

Military strategies employed by different factions to gain control of cities and countries varied, ranging from large-scale offensives to guerrilla warfare. Key ports and harbors became coveted targets due to their strategic importance for supply lines and naval operations.

This subchapter also examines the long-term effects of multiple occupations on the political landscape of cities and countries in the post-war era. Borders were redrawn, governments were toppled or installed, and power dynamics shifted, shaping the region's future for decades to come.

Shifting Borders: Eastern Europe's Turbulent Journey through World War II offers a comprehensive account of the challenges faced by civilians living in areas that were frequently occupied. It sheds light on the resilience and strength of these individuals, who not only survived but also contributed to the ultimate victory over tyranny.

For historians, educators, students, and the public, this subchapter provides a deeper understanding of the intricate tapestry of World War II in Eastern Europe, highlighting the often-overlooked stories of cities and countries that changed hands several times and the lasting impact of these power shifts.

The Soviet Sphere: Eastern Europe under Communist Rule

During World War II, Eastern Europe experienced significant turmoil as multiple countries and cities changed hands several times. One of the most notable outcomes of this period was the establishment of the Soviet Sphere, where Eastern European countries fell under Communist rule. This subchapter will delve into the impact of the Soviet Sphere on the region, focusing on its historical, social, economic, and political consequences.

Under Several Flags: A Historical Account of Cities and Countries that Changed Hands Several Times during World War II highlights the fluid nature of Eastern Europe's borders during this period. Cities such as Warsaw, Budapest, and Prague were repeatedly occupied by different factions, leading to immense destruction and loss of life. The chapter will shed light on the strategic importance of these key ports and harbors, which were fiercely contested due to their significance in transportation and military operations.

The Resistance Movements that emerged in these cities and countries played a crucial role in resisting the occupiers. These movements not only fought against the occupiers but also served as symbols of hope and unity for the local populations. The subchapter will explore their strategies, successes, and challenges faced by civilians living in areas that were frequently occupied.

The recurring occupations had a profound impact on the cultural, social, and economic fabric of the region. Local populations had to navigate multiple languages, ideologies, and political systems, leading to a complex social landscape. The chapter will delve into the long-term effects of these occupations, including the post-war political landscape and the establishment of Communist regimes in Eastern Europe.

Moreover, the economic consequences of frequent changes in ownership will be examined. The region's industrial infrastructure was severely damaged, and the subchapter will explore the efforts made to rebuild and recover from the war's devastation.

Addressing historians, educators, students, and the public, this subchapter aims to provide a comprehensive understanding of the Soviet Sphere's impact on Eastern Europe during World War II. By exploring the military strategies employed, the challenges faced by civilians, and the long-term consequences on political, cultural, and economic levels, readers will gain insight into this complex period of history. The chapter will also highlight lesser-known cities and regions that were heavily contested, shedding light on the diverse experiences of Eastern European populations during this turbulent era.

Legacy of Conflict: Lingering Tensions

Throughout Eastern Europe's turbulent journey through World War II, cities and countries were thrust into a perpetual cycle of changing hands. The subchapter "Legacy of Conflict: Lingering Tensions" delves deep into the profound impact of these multiple occupations on major European cities and regions. Addressing historians, educators, students, and the public, this chapter aims to shed light on the lesser-known aspects of this tumultuous period.

The strategic importance of key ports and harbors that were repeatedly captured during World War II cannot be overstated. These locations became battlegrounds, witnessing fierce clashes as different factions sought control. The military strategies employed by these factions to gain dominance over cities and countries are explored, highlighting the complexities of the conflict.

However, it is the resilience of the local populations that truly shapes the narrative. Resistance movements played a crucial role in cities and countries that changed hands multiple times. Their bravery and determination to defy occupiers resonated with the public, leaving an indelible mark on the cultural and social fabric of these regions.

The economic consequences of frequent changes in ownership during World War II cannot be ignored. The constant disruption of trade and commerce, coupled with the pillaging and destruction of resources, led to severe economic hardships for civilians living in these areas. The long-term effects of multiple occupations on the political landscape of cities and countries in the post-war era are also examined, providing a comprehensive understanding of the aftermath of this tumultuous period.

This chapter also sheds light on the challenges faced by civilians living in areas that were frequently occupied during World War II. Their daily lives were marred by fear, uncertainty, and the struggle to survive amidst the chaos of war. By examining the experiences of these individuals, we gain a deeper appreciation for the human cost of conflict.

"Legacy of Conflict: Lingering Tensions" is an important subchapter that touches upon various facets of Eastern Europe's journey through World War II. By exploring the impact on major cities, lesser-known regions, and the lives of civilians, this chapter offers a comprehensive understanding of the lingering tensions that stemmed from the frequent changes in ownership. It serves as a valuable resource for historians, educators, students, and the public, providing a nuanced perspective on this transformative period in history.

www.ingramcontent.com/pod-product-compliance
Lightning Source LLC
Chambersburg PA
CBHW021746150726
47989CB00004B/1540